What Our Readers Have Said...

"Although I consider myself a seasoned sales professional, it is helpful to have past learning's refreshed. The books were also beneficial because of the information concerning 'trends' in the sales relationship. The sales process should be viewed as dynamic since business relationships change regularly."

•

"For the particular business I am in and the type of sales calls I have, I find that the books in the Pinpoint Sales Training Series are very often applicable to how I conduct business. I would recommend them to other sales people, just not ones that are in my industry."

•

"These books provide very good concepts. It fits in well with the Bell Leadership training program that I attended in November."

•

"I use this material in these books and apply it to my customers and other employees I work with."

•

"I would like to know other topics. Is there anything on Production Management or Consultative Selling or Time Management?"

•

"These books are great tools that should be used as guidelines for our everyday

supervisory practices. You need to take the time to do a short self-evaluation when reading them."

•

"The Pinpoint Training Series delivers information that could be used in a lot different areas."

•

"I like this because I can take them with me to read at a convenient time. I feel the little time I have to spend in the office is best use on activities that directly relate to revenue opportunities. I like the short amount of time it takes to keep up with these."

•

"I prefer the self-study approach; it fits in with my schedule."

•

"My thought is that the real value of these books comes into effect when doing the action plans."

•

"Short and sweet. These books are easy to comprehend."

•

"I have enjoyed reading these books. They are relevant to today's work environment and the ongoing change in the way we manage our workforce."

•

"I do feel that these books have been very helpful to me at my job."

•

"I think a lot of the recommendations in these books are very useful, and can be applicable to everyday situations. If nothing else, it's a good reference guide to fall back upon if a situation arises in the future."

•

"These books are relevant to today's work environment and the ongoing change in the way we manage our workforce."

•

Innovative & Productive Sales Strategies

Pinpoint Sales Skill Development Training Series

TIMOTHY F. BEDNARZ

MAJORIUM
BUSINESS PRESS

Pinpoint Sales Skill Development Training Series
"Innovative & Productive Sales Strategies"
Timothy F. Bednarz

Graphic design: Monika Pawlak

Majorium Business Press
2025 Main Street
Stevens Point, WI 54481
715.342.1018 • 800.654.4935

ISBN 978-1-882181-93-3

Printed in the United States of America

Introduction

The Pinpoint Sales Skill Development Training Series is designed for targeted training and education regarding increased improvement in a specific skill or competency.

Each book within this series is designed to be easy to use, understand and apply to your job. It can be used as a basis for training individuals, as a discussion guide or as a personal training tool.

Each chapter within this book discusses a specific concept. When you have completed all eight chapters you should have a 360° perspective of the topic.

Additionally, each chapter is divided into specific sections:

- The first section provides you with an overview of the topic
- The Implications section discusses why the concept is important, and why it is important to learn and apply.
- The Strategies, Tips & Techniques to Apply section teaches how to use and apply the particular concept to your work.
- The Points to Ponder section gives you something to think about or to be discussed with a group setting. These are questions not meant to be immediately answered, but to be pondered over time.
- The Training Activity section provides you with the tools to transfer what you have learned to your job. It is designed to help create an action plan to effectively apply the concept.

Each of the topics in this series is time-tested and proven in the marketplace. They have been used by thousands of employees as training tools. Many of the users have commented that what made these books valuable, was the ability to refer to them when a problem surfaced. They indicated that they remembered reading about the exact problem. They referred back to these books and found an appropriate solution.

You will find them equally valuable as a resource in your professional development library.

Table of Contents

LEARNING OBJECTIVES:

- The need to be creative to gain a competitive advantage.
- How to use creative selling techniques to spark curiosity and a sense of urgency.
- How to build trust and credibility.
- How to make information tangible and meaningful to prospects.

1

Why Creative Selling Techniques Are Necessary?

One of the largest and most chronic problems being reported by salespeople is the inability to connect with prospects through either voicemail or email. Unfortunately, the electronic veil most prospects hide behind is a reality that salespeople must learn to work with and overcome. Unless salespeople talk to their with prospects, everything is an exercise in futility and frustration.

IMPLICATIONS – WHAT THIS MEANS TO YOU

Salespeople know their prospects are busy and that competition for their time is intense. They are vying with other salespeople, superiors and associates for their attention. When prospects review their email and voicemail, they are evaluating and prioritizing what they hear or see—and most is trashed without consideration. Consider a typical voicemail message that many salespeople leave:

Good Morning, This is John Smith from the XYZ Corporation. We are an innovative manufacturing company that has an exciting new production technology that I wanted to share with you. Please call me at 1-800... to learn how this program can greatly increase your company's effectiveness and results.

This voicemail may be varied and more intriguing from salesperson to salesperson, however, no matter how polished, it probably sounds like every other salesperson's voicemail. The result is the message is deleted without a call back. Some survey statistics indicate that only 2-5% of voicemail messages are returned. If salespeople hope to be successful, this is unacceptable.

STRATEGIES, TIPS & TECHNIQUES TO APPLY

Fortunately, salespeople can get better results with a change in how they approach their prospects. The key is to focus on and tap into a strong human tendency and motivator: curiosity.

Unless prospects are curious about what salespeople sell, no window exists to uncover their needs. In fact, curiosity is the genesis of every sale and the catalyst for every prospect to act. If salespeople are able to leverage curiosity, they can overcome the lack of callbacks. This will work because curious prospects will choose to engage salespeople to satisfy their curiosity.

The more curious prospects become, the more opportunities salespeople will have to add value and provide solutions. Curiosity is the key that unlocks the rest of the sales process. When prospects are curious and believe salespeople are credible, engaging them in a mutually beneficial business relationship becomes much easier.

Therefore, in order to differentiate themselves from the typical salesperson—not just to be different, but for the sake of getting results—salespeople must leverage curiosity to get more callbacks and ultimately engage more prospects in a productive sales conversation.

The key to leveraging a prospect's curiosity is not to think about features, benefits, solutions, needs, or relationships when leaving a voicemail message. Salespeople need to think about one thing and one thing only: what they can say that will make the prospect curious enough to call them back. The more curious prospects become, the sooner they call back.

Leveraging curiosity requires some thought and creativity, but there are many ways to do so. How salespeople go about it is up to them.

It should be noted that leveraging curiosity is not a manipulation strategy. Salespeople are not forcing or tricking prospects, but piquing their interest.

They are attempting to rise above the communications din and get themselves noticed. They are trying to initiate a conversation and see if it makes sense to engage further.

POINTS TO PONDER – SOMETHING TO THINK ABOUT

1. How well are you able to spark your prospects sufficiently to call you back, when leaving a voicemail?
2. Do you find the lack of adequate voicemail callbacks to be one of the most frustrating aspects of selling?

TRAINING ACTIVITY – APPLICATION & ACTION PLAN

Write out or review a written copy of your typical voicemail message(s).

1. Identify what in the message would spark the prospect's interest or make them curious enough to call you back.
2. Apply the "So What" test. When you have identified a curiosity inducing statement, ask the question, "So what?" and answer the question.
3. Determine whether your "So What" response provides a strong enough inducement for the prospect to call back or if it sounds like a generic statement every other salesperson might make.
4. Refine your message until you know that it will intrigue the prospect sufficiently to respond.

2

The Nine to Five Syndrome

What separates successful salespeople from average performers in most sales organizations? Often, the difference lies solely in individuals' perceptions and attitudes in relation to their jobs, tasks and responsibilities. Most average performers view their sales positions as simply "jobs" whereas successful people rightly view them as "professions that pay for results."

IMPLICATIONS — WHAT THIS MEANS TO YOU

Salespeople who perceive their jobs as nine-to-five positions shortchange the companies they work for as well as themselves. While many companies do hire scientists, engineers, accountants and other professionals to accomplish particular objectives, goals and missions, unlike any other jobs within them, salespeople are hired and judged solely on the results they are able to achieve. Just like these other professionals, the skills they learn and apply are directly transferable to other company positions and careers, as well as for advancing them in the ones they currently hold.

It is important for salespeople to understand that selling is a profession, not just a nine-to-five job to be forgotten when the workday is over. A regular job pays employees "time on the clock" for specific task completion, while selling pays for the results salespeople generate. Consequently, successful salespeople will be some of the highest paid people in most companies. Those who only consider selling to be "a job" should reconsider their perspectives and attitudes. If they are unable to change or dedicate themselves to higher levels of continuous personal involvement, they should definitely consider other careers or professions. Becoming a truly successful sales professional demands an investment of time, effort and commitment beyond the prime selling hours of nine to five.

STRATEGIES, TIPS & TECHNIQUES TO APPLY

Time—a limited resource—can become the salesperson's ally or enemy. This means that during prime selling hours their time should be carefully planned and maximized to include as much active "contact time" as possible. Two of the biggest stumbling blocks many salespeople run into are not sufficiently planning their time and activities for effective and efficient productivity, and actively wasting prime selling time by performing more non-productive tasks that could easily be accomplished on "off-the-clock" time.

Some specific areas that salespeople need to focus upon include:

Focus and Motivation

If salespeople want to obtain results, they must be focused on ways to achieve them. Any other focus deviates from their primary course of action. The motivation for success and the attainment of personal sales goals must come from a burning, driving force within salespeople, not from external sources such as sales managers' or company-related expectations.

When salespeople are internally focused and motivated, they do whatever they need to do to attain the results they want. Successful individuals continually strive to exceed goals and personal performance records. This benefits them financially and creates the means to successfully move their companies forward.

Dedication

Salespeople must be dedicated to their profession. This means not only doing what is necessary to succeed, but also taking the time to educate themselves about their own organizations in regard to targeted customers and industries as well as the market trends, problems and events that directly affect them. It also includes learning new skills and strategies that help them become professional experts and superior troubleshooters.

Highly successful salespeople use non-selling hours, including when they are traveling or other less productive time, to accomplish these tasks. They understand the importance of personal dedication because it makes them highly effective and extremely competent in their daily sales activities.

Preparation

The changing sales landscape and the increasing complexity of selling demands that salespeople invest more time to prepare themselves before contacting and meeting with prospective buyers. Most do not have the time or patience to deal with unprepared salespeople. If salespeople are unable to quickly identify and pinpoint areas of potential problems in order to spark a real interest, they will be quickly brushed off.

Salespeople must understand that it may take several hours of research to achieve the depth of knowledge required to successfully have enough information to formulate a message that is able to spark a particular prospect's interest and curiosity. It is unrealistic for salespeople to expect to be successful if they undertake their research and preparation during daily prime-time selling hours.

Housework

All salespeople are required to complete sales reports, expense documentation, and call reports as part of their normal sales responsibilities. To be more successful they should invest part of their evening hours or weekends to complete and file them so as not to cut into their prime selling contact hours.

Getting a Running Start

Salespeople who start each week and day wondering what they are going to do generally end up floundering and failing in their careers. Successful people have a plan established for each week before it begins. They know exactly what they need to do and when to do it. Additionally, they pull and review their account files for the week and invest the time to prepare for talking or meeting with new contacts. Plans may include researching particular company websites and using other informational resources to develop the knowledge needed to maximize their contact time. It often requires work over the weekends, but effective sales performers realize and recognize that extra planning and preparation is what directly contributes to their consistent success.

Salespeople who invest time in adequate preparation and planning quickly discover that their prime selling time becomes more productive, effective and fruitful. They find they can easily follow their plans and accomplish the specific goals they have established for the week. This is in contrast to more unprepared individuals who generally waste 50-75% of their prime selling time doing what could be accomplished during non-selling hours. It is little wonder many flounder and become frustrated.

Salespeople cannot hope to be successful if they only work nine to five. There is far too much to be accomplished. If they do limit themselves to general working hours, they subsequently limit their overall success as they simultaneously jeopardize their sales positions.

POINTS TO PONDER — SOMETHING TO THINK ABOUT

1. Do you personally perceive yourself as a professional salesperson, or merely one who does a job?
2. How much time outside of your prime selling hours do you typically devote to completing tasks, responsibilities and personal growth training and development? What is your attitude toward putting in the extra time? Why?

TRAINING ACTIVITY — APPLICATION & ACTION PLAN

Before you begin your sales week on Monday, adequately prepare the following items:

1. Your schedule of the week's sales activities
2. Goals and objectives for each planned sales activity
3. Required research and preparation for each sales activity
4. All the files and information you will need to refer to during the week

3

Before You Begin to Sell

Long gone are the days when salespeople could simply walk into a business "off the street" and take the needed time to educate potential buyers about their particular products or services. Today's prospects are much more pressed and harried, and salespeople need to earn the right to take their time. This can be accomplished if they prepare and develop comprehensive "prospect profiles" as the foundation for individual sales encounters and discussions. Many sales are won or lost solely by the amount of initial sales preparation that goes into the selling process.

IMPLICATIONS – WHAT THIS MEANS TO YOU

Today's prospective buyers have higher expectations of salespeople that correspond to the fast-paced market conditions they work within, including:

- They expect to deal with salespeople who are more knowledgeable than they are.
- They expect salespeople to know about their particular industries, businesses, products and customers.
- They expect salespeople to know more than they do about certain aspects of their respective industries and external customer needs.
- They expect salespeople to apply their expertise and experi-

ence and offer valuable information that helps solve pressing problems while providing methods, insights and applications to improve their businesses and give them a competitive advantage.

These expectations are important for salespeople to understand because the real value they bring into selling situations is their professional experience and expertise. With the narrowing of product space between competitive products and services, where there is little to distinguish one from another, it is what salespeople are personally able to bring to the table that often makes the difference in whether or not the sale is landed. It is the personal application of their unique expertise in regard to business-related problems and needs that builds and sustains their competitive advantage.

STRATEGIES, TIPS & TECHNIQUES TO APPLY

The success of moving sales to the point of closing hinges on the degree of preparation salespeople are willing to invest in initially developing their individual prospective accounts. A lack of preparation is more often than not what kills selling efforts before they even get off the ground. This is why it is essential for salespeople to prepare themselves on multiple levels.

The first level of preparation includes developing individual account profiles. Basic information about individual companies is researched before initial calls and encounters begin, which is subsequently placed into categorized folders that can be readily referenced. Making informational phone calls, personal visits or researching companies through the Internet can help glean valuable and necessary business account information.

Information at the initial level

- The prospective buyers' line of business—wholesale, retail, manufacturing, etc.
- The highest-ranking decision maker that the salesperson needs to access and address
- The level and title of the particular buyer(s) within the organization

- The final decision maker(s)
- Sales volume, number of employees, net worth, number and location of facilities
- How long the individual company has been in business
- Type of office location the salesperson will be calling on, such as branch, headquarters, etc.
- Reputation—known problems and successes
- Current relationship with the salesperson's company
- What the company's known goals and objectives are
- A list of factors that could present barriers to purchasing particular products or services
- Names of individuals who referred the salesperson to the contact person or company itself
- Any known problems or concerns the prospective buyer's company is experiencing as well as the specific requirements it has

When salespeople have a strong foundation of information about the particular companies they intend to contact, they are able to converse intelligently with prospective buyers about their specific needs, problems and concerns. Newspapers, company newsletters and trade journals are good supportive informational sources for company-related data, trends and insight.

Once salespeople begin to sell to individual accounts, there are additional levels of information that need to be developed.

Information about specific prospective buyers

- Names, ages, titles, positions, experience and years within the identified companies
- Their direct superiors
- Their buying authority
- Their personal styles
- Their professional reputations

- Their focus
- The needs, concerns or issues that are important to them personally as well as ones that are directly company-related
- Their particular goals and objectives
- Their current or past relationships with the salesperson's company

Additional qualifying information

- Product or service application(s)
- Competitive products or services each is currently using
- Current prices being paid for competitive products or services
- Volume of product used
- Problems with competitive products or services
- Overall problems not solved by competitive products or services
- Specific needs
- General budget and budget periods

This level and depth of information must be developed for every account salesperson attempting to sell. As they begin to build and establish solid business relationships, there will be additional levels of information that can be added to their individual account profiles.

Information is the lifeblood of selling. Salespeople cannot competently sell any accounts without gathering and applying in-depth information to combine with their experience and expertise, which is the only effective means for crafting highly credible, workable and efficient sales solutions.

POINTS TO PONDER — SOMETHING TO THINK ABOUT

1. What types of information do you research and develop in-depth before making your first call on a particular prospect? Explain.
2. What has been your experience with specific levels of account information? What do you feel defines an "optimal account profile"?

TRAINING ACTIVITY — APPLICATION & ACTION PLAN

1. Based upon your professional experience, develop an outline that specifically details the various types of information you need in order to successfully sell a particular account.
2. Include the information you require and the questions you need to ask to fully develop this information.
3. Detail the sources you need to use to generate this information.

4

Sparking Prospect's Curiosity

Salespeople know their prospects are busy and that competition for their time is intense. When prospects review their email and voicemail, they are evaluating and prioritizing what they hear or see, and most is deleted without consideration.

IMPLICATIONS — WHAT THIS MEANS TO YOU

Salespeople are doing that which every other salesperson is doing: leaving voicemails that are polished, but sound alike and fail to spark the prospect's curiosity. Rather than rising above the electronic din, they are directly in the midst of it.

Rather than step back and examine what is happening, most salespeople will continue to call 10, 20, 30 or 50 times without seeing an increase in sales activity. Rather than appear professional, they become collective pests. This applies to the vast majority of salespeople.

Curiosity is the key that unlocks the rest of the sales process. When prospects are curious and believe salespeople are credible, it becomes easy to engage them in a mutually beneficial business relationship.

STRATEGIES, TIPS & TECHNIQUES TO APPLY

There are five things that can be used to induce a prospect's curiosity.

Provocative Questions and Statements

Provocative questions and statements tend to make prospects curious. They wonder why salespeople asked what they did. Examples of these statements include: "Guess what?" and "Can I ask you a question?"

Partial Information

Many salespeople spend a considerable amount of time attempting to satisfy the prospect's curiosity and very little time creating it. They assume that their value lies in the information they provide. If salespeople agree that curiosity is the key to unlock the rest of the sales process, then satisfying prospects' curiosity actually eliminates the incentive for prospects to engage further. If prospects' curiosity is satisfied during the initial meeting, what is their incentive to schedule another meeting or call? There is no reason to follow up.

Rather than telling everything up front, salespeople need to share only enough information to pique prospects' curiosity and communicate value, but not so much that they remove their incentive to move to the next step of the sales process.

Glimpses of Value

Another way to pique a prospect's curiosity is to use glimpses of value. Dangling valuable benefits in front of prospects entices them to want more information.

"Mr. Smith, if our model 343 increased your plant's productivity and enabled it to average an additional 8% profit, for less than you are currently paying, would you be interested? Would you like me to show you how?"

"Other companies are realizing significant increases in productivity and effectiveness. Would you like to know how much?"

Most prospects want to know how to save money, increase productivity and get a return on their investment. By providing glimpses of value to them, this piques their interest and sparks their curiosity.

This technique can be used to identify problems and indicate to prospects that salespeople have the solution. Bringing up the biggest challenges early in the conversation can do this.

"Do you find that your salespeople need to continually polish their skills and learn new techniques and ideas to solve difficult problems? Would you like to learn how we've overcome this challenge?"

When prospects find out that salespeople may be able to solve their problems, they will become curious and want to know more. Essentially salespeople are asking, "If I could show you how to improve your existing condition, would you be interested in taking the next step?"

Newness and Exclusivity

New things are exciting and people always want to be "in the know." This affords an excellent opportunity to engage new prospects and reengage old ones.

"We have pioneered a new production technology that can directly impact your business. I wanted to see if it would make sense to bring you up to speed?"

In this manner, by engaging in an in-depth discussion of prospects' needs and solutions, salespeople can communicate that their program is valuable to their business.

Leveraging Momentum

People are affected by the herd effect, or when they think others are moving in a specific direction. This is a high impact method to induce curiosity and capture prospects' attention. This leverages salespeople's credibility. When "everyone else" is already moving in a certain direction, prospects will become curious as to why.

"Companies like IBM, Cisco, Sprint, and Gateway have benefited from our products. *Fortune* and *Business Week* have featured our products in their magazines and companies like ADP, Corporate Express, Kohler, and Farmers' Manufacturing are considering our process. Would you like to learn why?"

While certain salespeople do not yet have a marquee list of customers, they can refer to companies that have used their programs as pilots, are strong prospects and have positively evaluated their programs.

POINTS TO PONDER — SOMETHING TO THINK ABOUT

1. What techniques do you successfully use to pique a prospect's interest?
2. Do you tend to "tell it all" in the first meeting, leaving nothing for prospects to be curious about?

TRAINING ACTIVITY — APPLICATION & ACTION PLAN

Listed below are the five techniques that you can use to create curiosity:

- Provocative Questions and Statements
- Partial Information
- Glimpses of Value
- Newness and Exclusivity
- Leveraging Momentum

1. For each technique, create at least one statement that you can use to pique a prospect's interest.
2. Review each and determine the strength and power of each statement.
3. Polish and manipulate each statement to create a powerful statement.
4. Identify where and when each statement should be used.

5

Creating a Sense of Urgency

The identification of a prospect's needs is fundamental to the success of every salesperson. If prospects don't recognize their own needs, they will be unable to recognize the value of the products or services presented to them. Without recognition of their needs, prospects will fail to develop a sense of urgency to make an immediate purchase.

IMPLICATIONS – WHAT THIS MEANS TO YOU

Salespeople can struggle with the ability to create a strong sense of urgency that motivates prospects to buy. Many are frustrated by this inability, but this demonstrates a real need to improve their sales skills because the salesperson's ability to transform complacency into urgency is what selling is all about.

Salespeople must understand that it is natural for prospects to be comfortable with the status quo. Change is equated with extra work and risk that most prospects don't want to contend with. They fail to understand that the risks can be greater when they don't take action. The role of salespeople must be to educate their prospects to realize that they can't take advantage of the opportunities they are unaware of. Otherwise, they are doomed to fail, because uninformed prospects are much less likely to make a favorable buying decision.

Salespeople understand that there are two types of needs in the marketplace:

Active Needs

Active needs occur when prospects recognize their dissatisfaction or discontent with their existing solution or the status quo. Prospects with active needs have immediate needs. Sales cycles are shorter and buying decisions are made more quickly. Unfortunately these highly desirable prospects represent only between 5-10% of the market.

Latent Needs

Latent needs exist when prospects fail to recognize that they are no longer satisfied with their existing solution or status quo. The primary reason latent needs exist is ignorance. When prospects are unaware of a problem, they have no reason to upset the status quo. While their needs may be real, they have a false sense of security. Consequently, there is no sense of urgency to make a change.

The majority of sales prospects fall in the latent needs category. It is the responsibility of salespeople to uncover points of pain and discontent that identify these needs and then educate the prospects about the problem and its consequences. Only when this occurs can the prospect's perspective be changed. When this happens, a sense of urgency is created. When salespeople transform latent into active needs, this escalates the prospect's sense of urgency to find and identify a solution. When this happens, the salesperson's probability of making the sale improves dramatically.

Complacency

There is a small likelihood for success when salespeople dangle potential solutions in front of prospects with latent needs. No matter how superior the solutions salespeople offer, these prospects will not be interested in them since they see no need for them.

This results in a sense of complacency because prospects are already satisfied with the status quo. The benefits of a new solution are not outweighed by a need to make a change.

Urgency

A sense of urgency motivates prospects to take action to alleviate the source of pain and discontent. The greater the prospect's sense of urgency, the more likely they are to act on the solutions presented to them. For salespeople to achieve a sense of urgency in their prospects, they must transform their needs from latent to active through a process of mutual discovery, where they are educated about the consequences of their inaction. As prospects move from ignorance to pain and discontent with their current situation, their perspective of the situation changes from complacency to urgency. As salespeople offer new information or ask questions to probe prospects' situations, they are lead to discover specific opportunities that improve their existing condition. Salespeople are able to use these methods to raise awareness.

While many salespeople are reluctant to do this for fear of being too intrusive, they should realize that they are doing prospects a service by providing valuable solutions that they may otherwise not have been aware of.

POINTS TO PONDER – SOMETHING TO THINK ABOUT

1. Have you been frustrated by an inability to create a sense of urgency in prospects?
2. Do you focus prospects on the consequences of inaction or a choice not to act on new opportunities?

TRAINING ACTIVITY — APPLICATION & ACTION PLAN

Identify five prospects that you feel you are incapable of creating a sense of urgency in.

1. Identify both the active and latent needs in each account.
2. If unable to identify active and latent needs, develop a series of questions that assist prospects to uncover their needs.
3. If unaware of the points of pain and discontent, focus on the areas of superiority and differentiation that your product or service delivers.
4. Spend time to work with prospects to uncover their needs that can change their perspective.
5. Determine the consequences of inaction once you have uncovered the prospects needs.

6

Establishing Credibility

The best way for salespeople to establish credibility for themselves is through their ability to leverage existing relationships. This is why networking and developing active referral networks is stressed. In reality many salespeople struggle to establish credibility with prospects where no relationship exists.

IMPLICATIONS — WHAT THIS MEANS TO YOU

Salespeople without a relationship to leverage will often attempt to build a strong impression with the prospect by making claims of greatness about their company, products and services. Unfortunately these claims will put prospects in a defensive posture. It makes them more cautious and undermines salespeople's ability to establish trust and rapport. This is because prospects quickly make immediate judgments about their salespeople. This is often based upon the statements and claims they make and the questions that they ask.

Many of the sales techniques being used by most salespeople are also being used by the competition. These existing techniques immerse salespeople into the great mass of competition that completely eliminates their ability to differentiate themselves.

STRATEGIES, TIPS & TECHNIQUES TO APPLY

One way salespeople can establish credibility is to manage the scope, or the broadness or narrowness of their questions. Salespeople are trained to use open-ended questions with prospects to encourage them to "open up." While this method is effective, salespeople should recognize that the vast majority of prospects are reluctant to share their feelings and open up to salespeople until they have established their credibility. Most prospects feel that salespeople have extremely low levels of credibility, so this is the initial hurdle to overcome.

One large mistake many salespeople make is probing prospects too quickly. Without personal credibility, prospects will be reluctant to share information until salespeople have earned the right to ask questions. This can be overcome when salespeople demonstrate high levels of competence and credibility by narrowing the scope of their questions.

When salespeople demonstrate the ability to ask intelligent and relevant questions, prospects will automatically perceive a higher level of competence, credibility and value. This can be done with the use of closed-ended and specific diagnostic questions. They are intentionally concise and easy to answer. Brevity at this stage is critical because salespeople have a limited amount of time to pique the prospect's curiosity and establish credibility. This makes diagnostic questions valuable sales tools. Examples can include:

"How many production machines are you running?"

"Are these machines located in a single location?"

"How many units do they produce in an hour?"

"What products are you using in these machines?"

Diagnostic questions effectively gather valuable information that qualifies the prospect while demonstrating the salesperson's expertise concerning the application. When salespeople demonstrate that they know how to ask intelligent and relevant diagnostic questions, they communicate higher levels of competence, credibility and value. This allows salespeople to distinguish themselves from the competition that use sweeping claims to establish their credibility.

The use of diagnostic questions engages prospects and creates curiosity and credibility. Once salespeople establish their credibility, they have earned the right to broaden the scope of their questions and probe their thoughts, feelings and concerns. When prospects are curious and believe salespeople are credible, it is easy to uncover their needs and present solutions. They will have overcome their personal reluctance to answer questions since salespeople have established and proven their credibility.

The key to the use of diagnostic questions is to start with broad questions. This allows salespeople to view the big picture and to probe more deeply into specific areas. Additionally salespeople should provide prospects with choices when using these questions. When salespeople offer prospects choices, they make the questions easier to answer.

Salespeople should be both relevant and interesting. When they narrow the scope of questions, salespeople are helping prospects break down large and often intimidating decisions into easier to handle component parts.

Salespeople should understand that closed-ended questions are excellent ways to build credibility, but are not effective for building relationships. Salespeople must also be aware of when to make the transition into open-ended questions that uncover prospect's needs.

POINTS TO PONDER – SOMETHING TO THINK ABOUT

1. Do you have a tendency to probe your prospects before you establish your credibility?
2. What has been the result when you have failed to initially establish credibility with prospects?

TRAINING ACTIVITY — APPLICATION & ACTION PLAN

Take time to discuss with fellow sales associates or non-competitive colleagues the questions they use with their prospects.

1. Compile a list of most frequently asked questions.
2. Observe the similarities in the questions that are asked regardless of the industry.
3. Develop your own list of diagnostic questions.
4. Memorize these questions and practice them until you are able to comfortably ask them.

7

Presenting Too Much Information

Salespeople must be careful not to hurt their chances of securing an order by presenting too much information early on in the sales process. When they tend to communicate everything they know up front, there is no compelling reason for prospects to continue discussions. The element of curiosity has been removed, along with the impetus to want to hear more about specific product or service applications and benefits.

IMPLICATIONS – WHAT THIS MEANS TO YOU

Salespeople have the obligation to uncover business-related problems and attached negative ramifications for prospects to weigh and consider. Most of these have financial costs associated with them. Salespeople who are able to identify these costs early on are in a better position to justify the value of their particular solutions in the formal selling process.

If salespeople are unable to discover the true costs that are directly attributable to particular business-related problems, prospects will not understand the inherent value their offerings provide. Therefore, salespeople must be able to develop fully researched and customized presentations that consistently refer to the effects and drains of hidden costs, as well as those caused by a failure to make positive changes. These hidden costs must be compared against actual purchase prices. The problem is salespeople often rely on generic pitches to sell their products or services when customized presentations are needed to highlight these hidden costs.

STRATEGIES, TIPS & TECHNIQUES TO APPLY

Salespeople should be careful when presenting sales-related information. Listing features and benefits is not enough to stimulate curiosity and a feeling of urgency when it comes to prospects addressing their problems and ongoing frustrations. This is because the technological advances available today easily duplicate features, functions and ease of use capabilities, which numerous competitors are generally able to offer as well.

Instead, salespeople need to identify ways they can uniquely help to identify, establish and attain prospects' business-related goals. Up to this point, prospects are often focused on whether to buy, not what to buy. The main objective is to move them forward by designing unique solutions to meet their specific needs and requirements, which simultaneously overcome most of their pressing issues and concerns. The ability to do this effectively is what aids salespeople in differentiating themselves from competitors. Uniquely devised options and alternatives are extremely difficult to replicate or match. Major orders often hinge on minor differences. Salespeople must make certain to point out all the various inherent specialized features, conveniences, advantages and capabilities, no matter how minor they may seem.

Flooding prospects with information and proposals before they are ready to consider it is completely counterproductive. Such an approach suggests that salespeople are solely focused on getting through the selling process and to their commission as fast as possible. It becomes obvious that meeting needs and requirements is far down on their lists of priorities. Immediately bombarding prospects with a sea of material, facts, data, numbers and supportive documentation greatly undermines the mutual establishment of trust, rapport and relationship cementing.

Professional salespeople know the importance of taking the time to uncover pressing but hidden needs and putting in the extra effort to establish feasible solutions on a case-by-case prospect basis. Once a specific need is fully recognized, weighed and considered, most prospects will become curious about possible solutions and alternatives. However, most will still want to research all options before making an actual purchasing decision. This is why salespeople need to be in constant contact throughout this phase—or risk losing control of the process. If too much information is detailed and quickly provided, prospects may choose to research options independently or with other competitors. The initial detailed information can easily be used as a means of bargaining or leveraging a better deal, or worse yet, competitors can use it to come in with initial counteroffers that are too strong to re-compete against.

To prevent this from occurring, salespeople must be careful to pace the delivery of their information. The ideal point to deliver key facts and extremely powerful specific product or service information is after prospects have conducted all the research possible and looked at all available alternatives. The timing of delivering key information assures that it will be compared against all other options. If salespeople are able to present their information once extensive research has been conducted, prospects will be better informed and more capable of intelligently and thoroughly evaluating the real and true value their particular offerings provide.

POINTS TO PONDER – SOMETHING TO THINK ABOUT

1. Have you lost an order to a competitor who used your work to his or her advantage by researching and matching a solution you presented? Explain what happened and the lessons you have learned.
2. Are you fully capable of creating unique sales solutions based upon your competitive differences? Explain.

TRAINING ACTIVITY – APPLICATION & ACTION PLAN

1. Identify a major prospect you are currently working with.
2. Develop a unique solution based upon your competitive advantages.
3. Develop a presentation schedule to pace the delivery of information that you need to provide to your particular prospect.

8

Make It Tangible

All salespeople are familiar with the features and benefits of their products. However, they tend to focus on tangible benefits rather than on the intangible ones. This is a tactical mistake. Most competitive product features are increasingly similar with little to differentiate one product from another.

Smart salespeople use intangible benefits to create a product space to differentiate their product from the competition. They understand how to quantify these benefits and what needs to be done to clearly demonstrate how these intangible benefits impact the prospect.

IMPLICATIONS – WHAT THIS MEANS TO YOU

Most individuals have a difficult time visualizing intangible items, chiefly because they are often difficult to define and attach a financial benefit to. Yet, in most sales situations it is the intangibles that can clinch the sale. It is also because most tangible benefits are so similar with the host of "me-too" products in the marketplace that it becomes difficult for customers to distinguish one product from another.

By making intangible benefits tangible, salespeople will be capable of building a strong case for the customer to buy from them. It will be difficult for the competition to counter, as most intangible benefits tend to be unique and most others will not be able to take the time to specifically quantify them.

STRATEGIES, TIPS & TECHNIQUES TO APPLY

The problem for many salespeople is they fail to understand how to quantify an intangible benefit. It's not normally a benefit that would be associated with the product. More often, the benefit is simply taken for granted. It takes a certain amount of creativity to pause and think outside of the typical sales situational box.

The following techniques can be useful in defining the intangible benefits a product has to offer.

Salespeople need to understand the customer always seeks the answer to the question, "What's in it for me?" All sales strategies should be built around an approach that provides comprehensive answers to this critical question.

1. Salespeople need to identify and determine what an intangible benefit means to the customer in terms of added time, convenience, profits, etc. In other words, "You'll receive this benefit, which means you will get… This typically will be something of value that the customer may not automatically think of or associate as a savings when using the product.
2. Salespeople should reinforce the intangible benefit's importance with hard facts. Quantify and document wherever possible. Once a value has been established, it is easy to establish a worth to the customer and what the value actively provides to them.
3. Salespeople need to relate the facts to the benefits that would be derived if the customer orders their product or service. By linking an intangible benefit to an established monetary value, the salesperson has essentially made an intangible benefit tangible in the customer's mind. In this way, customers have been educated as to the additional value the product offers them in competitive product areas. This widens the product space and provides the salesperson with a competitive advantage.

It should be noted that it takes time and creative effort to view a product from a number of varying perspectives before distinct intangible benefits can be identified. Additionally, it takes creative thinking to identify and quantify the costs and value associated with intangible benefits. However, once established, these intangible benefits can be repeatedly used in sales presentations to differentiate the product from the competition.

POINTS TO PONDER – SOMETHING TO THINK ABOUT

1. Have you ever used intangible benefits to differentiate your product from the competition?
2. Can you think of instances when intangible benefits can be used to your advantage over your competitors?

TRAINING ACTIVITY – APPLICATION & ACTION PLAN

1. Select one major product and identify the intangible benefits. It might be useful to brainstorm with other salespeople.
2. Once you have identified the intangible benefits, quantify each benefit and establish a value.
3. Link the intangible benefit to the established value and build a sales scenario to use when presenting these benefits to your customers.

About the Author

Timothy F. Bednarz, Ph.D. is CEO of the American Management Development Group, Inc. For over 20 years he has researched, designed and authored hundreds of learning and development programs used by Fortune 1000 companies.

He is also the author of *Great! What Makes Leaders Great. What They Did, How They Did It and What You Can Learn from It* (2011).

Speaking Availability

Timothy F. Bednarz, Ph.D. is available for speaking engagements for your next meeting or association event. He can be contacted at 800-654-4935 or by e-mail at timothy.bednarz@majorium.com.

Bulk Sales

Bulk sales of this book or any other titles available from Majorium Business Press. Inquiries can be directed to sales@majorium.com, or by phone at 800-6654-4935.

Quick Order Form

Fax orders: 715-342-1118. Send this form.

Telephone orders: Call 800-654-4935 toll-free. Have your credit card ready.

Email orders: sales@majorium.com

Postal orders: Majorium Business Press, 2025 Main Street, Stevens Point, WI 54481, USA.

Please send the following books:

____

____

____

____

Please send more FREE information on:

❑Catalog ❑Speaking/Seminars ❑Mailing Lists ❑Consulting

Name: ____

Address: ____

City: _______________________ State: _____ Zip: _________

Telephone: ____

Email address: ______________________________________

Sales tax: Please add 5.5% for products shipped to Wisconsin addresses.

Shipping by air:

United States: $4.00 for first book and $2.00 for each additional product.

International: $9.00 for first book; $5.00 for each additional product (estimate).

Made in United States
Cleveland, OH
06 November 2026

47678342R10030

Made in United States
Cleveland, OH
06 November 2026

47678361R10030